THE DIRECTOR

Nancy Hasty

BROADWAY PLAY PUBLISHING INC
New York
www.broadwayplaypublishing.com
info@broadwayplaypublishing.com

THE DIRECTOR
© Copyright 2001 by Nancy Hasty

All rights reserved. This work is fully protected under the copyright laws of the United States of America. No part of this publication may be photocopied, reproduced, stored in a retrieval system, or transmitted, in any form or by any means, electronic, mechanical, recording, or otherwise, without the prior permission of the publisher. Additional copies of this play are available from the publisher.

Written permission is required for live performance of any sort. This includes readings, cuttings, scenes, and excerpts. For amateur and stock performances, please contact Broadway Play Publishing Inc. For all other rights contact the author c/o B P P I.

Cover photo by Joan Marcus
First printing: October 2001
I S B N: 978-0-88145-195-5
Book design: Marie Donovan
Page make-up: Adobe Indesign
Typeface: Palatino
Copy editing: Sue Gilad
Printed and bound in the U S A

The author gratefully acknowledges the following people who assisted in the development of THE DIRECTOR: Claire McGill, Elizabeth Perry, Constance Ahlin, Janis Efronson, David Rothenberg, Rachel Falk, Byron Loyd, Sean Haggerty, Gayton Scott, Cameron Miller, Marja Adriance, Christopher Cartmill, Penny Balfour, Stephanie Cannon, Michael Griffiths, Phillip Clark, Margit Ahlin, Al D'Andrea, The American Renaissance Theater Co, The New Voice Theater Company, The Actors Lab, the Hasty family—and a special thanks to Tim Monsion.

THE DIRECTOR was originally developed by New Voice Theater. It was then produced by Laine Valentino and Kate Wachter at the Arclight Theater, opening on 15 February 2000 and running until 1 July. The opening cast and creative contributors were:

PETER	John Shea
ANNIE	Tasha Lawrence
MEG	Tanya Clark
BARNEY	Warren Press
JOHN	Todd Simmons
SALLY	Shula Van Buren
Director	Evan Bergman
Set	John Farrell
Costumes	Jill Kliber
Lighting	Steve Rust
Stage manager	Rebecca Wilson

CHARACTERS & SETTING

PETER
ANNIE
MEG
BARNEY
JOHN
SALLY

The play takes place in a run-down New York City rehearsal studio. The time is the present.

This play is dedicated to my niece
Claire Ashleigh McGill
with love and gratitude

ACT ONE

Scene One

(Lights rise on a small, cluttered room in a rehearsal studio. There are books everywhere, crammed into bookshelves, piled on chairs, stacked on the floor. In one corner is an unmade cot and in the other, a makeshift kitchen consisting of a half-refrigerator and a hot plate. There is an airshaft outside the tiny window and posters of philosophers and musicians are taped to the peeling walls. Sitting at a small table, sipping a cup of tea and reading, is PETER. *In his mid-forties,* PETER *is a fine figure of a man, appearing both rugged and poetic at the same time. He wears work clothes and at least two dozen keys jingle from a chain on his belt.)*

(Outside his room, we see ANNIE *approaching. In her late thirties, she is an attractive, intelligent woman, and at the moment appears both nervous and intense. She starts to knock, stops, then starts to knock again. She waits, summons up her courage, and finally raps on* PETER's *door.)*

PETER: Who is it?

*(*ANNIE, *not hearing* PETER, *knocks again—louder.)*

PETER: *Who is it?*

*(*ANNIE *freezes. A moment later the door opens slightly.)*

PETER: What?

ANNIE: Oh, hi. I hate to bother you—Peter, right? I'm Annie Sanders. We're rehearsing on the second floor and—

PETER: Whatever it is, you'll have to talk to Michael. He's downstairs.

ANNIE: I did. He told me you were up here.

PETER: Sorry, I'm off. You need to go to Michael, okay?

(PETER *starts to close the door.* ANNIE *stops him.*)

ANNIE: It's not about space or rooms or anything.

PETER: What is it?

ANNIE: Could I offer you a drink by any chance—or maybe a cup of coffee?

PETER: No, thanks. I'm afraid I'm busy.

ANNIE: *(In a rush)* I'm bothering you and that's the last thing I wanted to do. I'll make this quick. The bottom line is, I think I know you.

(PETER *pauses, waiting.*)

ANNIE: I mean I don't *know-you*, know-you. But if you're who I think you are, I've met you before and I know *of* you. *(Pause)* Can I come in just for a minute?

(PETER *widens the door and allows* ANNIE *to enter. She glances quickly around his room.*)

ANNIE: Oh, my goodness. Is this where you…

PETER: This is my lair, my den of iniquity…I'm the phantom of the rehearsal hall.

ANNIE: I wasn't making fun.

PETER: I was. Now, how do you know me?

ANNIE: Well, this is such a long shot, but you look so much like a director that came to my college almost fifteen years ago with a group of actors from Australia. Was that you?

PETER: You think you saw me fifteen years ago—where? Doing what?

ANNIE: You were doing *Macbeth*. In Denver.

ACT ONE

PETER: Me! Directing *Macbeth*, in Denver? *(Pause)* Why, yes, I believe I was.

ANNIE: I knew it! All week, every time I saw you I'd think, that's him. And then I'd go, no, it can't be. But it is. How about that! And you gave a talk afterwards. To the theater majors. We were blown away. Someone who'd trained with Grotowski! Ahhh!

PETER: I was having a cup of tea. Would you care for some?

ANNIE: I would love some. But I really didn't mean to—

PETER: Yes, you did. *(He smiles.)* Sit.

(As PETER *turns away to make the tea,* ANNIE *sits and takes in the books, the posters, and a stack of Carnegie Hall programs. She rifles through the programs.)*

ANNIE: My God, did you go to all these concerts?

PETER: I'm afraid so.

ANNIE: You really like the piano, don't you?

PETER: I should.

ANNIE: Why?

PETER: I used to play.

ANNIE: Really? Classical piano? Really?

PETER: So. You saw *Macbeth* and I gave a speech and you were blown away. And who in the hell are you— Annie? Annie what?

ANNIE: Sanders. Can I just say one more thing about *Macbeth*? I've never seen a better production—ever.

PETER: Thank you.

ANNIE: It was so real. That's what I remember most. It was so *real*. And the things you did! The way you had Lady Macbeth double as one of the witches! That scene where they were circling him and laughing at him and looked up and recognized her and the way he just kept blinking his eyes like he couldn't believe it—

PETER: Would you like milk?

ANNIE: No, that's fine.

(PETER *hands her a mug and sits opposite her.*)

ANNIE: By the way, your Lady Macbeth was brilliant. They all were, but when she was onstage it was like—like...

PETER: Hearing the angels sing.

ANNIE: Yes. How did you get that kind of performance?

PETER: I can't claim credit for talent like that. Her gift was from God.

ANNIE: Well, you directed it. It was one of my best memories. And here you are!

PETER: *(Looking about the room)* Yes, here I am.

ANNIE: *(Embarrassed)* Lemon! I love lemon!

PETER: So I gave a speech. God.

ANNIE: On the Theater of Cruelty and Antonin Artaud and his views on acting and how actors shouldn't be trying to "get" anything. That their only need should be to give. I remember your exact words. They should be like people dying...they should be like people burning...

PETER: Victims! They should be like "victims burnt at the stake, signaling through the flames."

ANNIE: Hey, the actors in my play should hear that speech! Could you come down tomorrow around three?

PETER: Sorry. I don't give speeches anymore.

ANNIE: Peter, if you don't mind my asking, what are you doing these days?

ACT ONE

PETER: I think that's obvious. I'm the janitor.

ANNIE: What do you mean?

PETER: I work the day shift and Michael lets me live here—rent free.

ANNIE: I think that that's a crime. I think that's an absolute crime.

PETER: And at night, I study.

ANNIE: *(Glancing at the books)* I see.

PETER: No, not with books. I study acting. With actors. I have my own theater.

ANNIE: You do? Where?

PETER: Right here. After midnight, this whole building is mine. I can work all night if I choose. I told you—I'm the phantom of the rehearsal hall! Thank you for your concern, but the work goes on.

ANNIE: I'm glad. But who would want to work all night?

PETER: Actors who are committed to the work, not to a clock.

ANNIE: I see. What are you directing now?

PETER: I don't direct anymore. I haven't directed in years.

ANNIE: But you just said—

PETER: I said I *study* acting. I experiment, that's all. I explore. And you—just what is it you do?

ANNIE: I teach.

PETER: No, I mean here.

ANNIE: Oh, here? What am I doing here? My play! We're working on my play. This is it. *(She pulls a script out of her bag.)*

PETER: Hmmm. *(Reading) Riding Out the Storm.* Good title. There's music in it. What do you teach?

ANNIE: Theater history—at Missouri State. Or rather, I did. It's so trite, isn't it? You write a play, win an award, and then quit your job and move to New York City.

PETER: I don't know—all or nothing.

ANNIE: All or nothing. All or nothing...that's from a play.

PETER: Ibsen.

ANNIE: *Master Builder?*

PETER: *Brand.*

ANNIE: *Brand*! That's right. It was all or nothing and then he was killed in an avalanche. Like me! We open in two weeks.

PETER: Where?

ANNIE: On Theater Row—a playwrights' festival. God, I've got to get back.

PETER: Don't let me keep you.

ANNIE: Wish you would. I hate what they're doing to it. They're ruining it. Well, thanks. This has been the highlight. It's not often you find the people again who inspired you. *(Extending her hand)* Really. Thanks.

PETER: Thank you. I enjoyed it. Oh! Don't forget your play.

ANNIE: It's an extra. Keep it! You might need to stuff your sock!

(ANNIE *exits.* PETER *closes the door and begins reading her script as the lights fade to black.)*

(End of Scene One)

ACT ONE

Scene Two

(It is two days later.)

(Lights rise in a rehearsal studio. ANNIE *is ripping masking tape up from the floor as* PETER, *carrying a broom and industrial trash can, enters.)*

PETER: Finished?

ANNIE: Peter!

PETER: Annie.

ANNIE: I didn't see you yesterday. I was worried I'd talked you into your grave.

PETER: I was sleeping. I stayed up all night reading…

ANNIE: You're a reader all right.

PETER: Your play.

ANNIE: Oh.

PETER: It's about your family, isn't it? It really happened?

ANNIE: Yes.

PETER: Kate is your sister.

ANNIE: Was.

PETER: She did kill herself?

ANNIE: Just the way it's written.

PETER: And Kate and the other sister, Ellen, were really rivals for that farmhand—Vincent?

(As ANNIE *nods.)*

PETER: Do you know which sister I like the best? The youngest one—

ANNIE: Susie.

PETER: *(Smiling)* Susie. And the image of a nine-year-old riding her bike all those miles through a storm—God, what guts.

ANNIE: I had to get there. She needed me.

PETER: When did you write it?

ANNIE: Last year. Want to hear something weird? I wrote it in the dark. I sat in the dark with my eyes closed and just listened to their voices. Take *that* to therapy. I think I was trying to bring them back.

PETER: You did.

ANNIE: Peter...did you...like it?

PETER: Very much.

ANNIE: You don't know how much that means—coming from you. I don't know anymore what to think of it. The rehearsals are terrible. The actors are miscast. The director is an asshole! He just doesn't get it.

PETER: Then find someone good. Your play deserves it.

ANNIE: All right then, I'll ask you. Will you direct my play?

PETER: No.

ANNIE: Why not?

PETER: I told you, I don't direct anymore.

ANNIE: Would you want to *study* it? You know, late at night, with some actors?

PETER: Annie, believe me. You don't want me. You're looking for something I can't give you. In Australia we rehearsed Ibsen's *Brand* for almost a year and we finally did it for about ten people. I don't care if ten people see what I do, or no one. You want a commercial run of your play that will please an audience and get good reviews, right?

ANNIE: No! I want you to work on it—if you will—and make it come to life!

PETER: It's impossible.

ANNIE: Why?

ACT ONE

PETER: Because I ask the impossible. My only interest is in the doing. To break through boundaries. To bend reality. To make something real. That's it. The rest of it I gave up long ago.

ANNIE: But listen—

PETER: Annie, it's no use.

ANNIE: Peter, do you believe in God? Or fate?

PETER: Annie, it's no use!

ANNIE: Just listen to me. It's too many coincidences. There's something at work here. Something I can't even comprehend. But listen! We've met before. We meet again. You just said you study plays, I need a director. You like my play, I *love* your direction—

PETER: Annie, another reason it's impossible is because *I'm* impossible. I become obsessed. I'm a dictator. I can be a real bastard. There's only one actor in the whole world who still wants to work with me. Before I came here, I was in San Diego, before that I was in Canada, before that I was in Denver, before that, Australia…

ANNIE: Peter, what if it wasn't impossible? What if you didn't have to work in the dead of night? What if you had this room every single day for as long as you needed it? What if you had help, real help, in finding the right actors. What if it was possible? Would you want to work on my play—as a real play—as a possible production—however long it takes? Would you? *(Pause)* Would you?

(PETER *shakes his head, crosses away from* ANNIE, *and stands lost in thought. Then, suddenly, he picks up a chair and with great precision places it center stage.*)

PETER: In your play, Kate's chair should be there. And behind the chair would be the hallway. Not over on the side. Directly behind the chair. And the hallway is long, very, very long. Sit in the chair, you're Kate.

Don't turn around! And you're waiting for Vincent. I'm the aunt. I'm starting down the hall behind you. You can't see me, but you can feel me coming. You can feel me coming for a long, long time.

(PETER *tip-toes behind* ANNIE *and then grabs her shoulders, causing her to squeal in excitement.*)

ANNIE: Oh, my God, especially in the first scene when she thinks Aunt Rose is asleep.

PETER: But she's not asleep. She's creeping down the hall—

ANNIE: A *long* hall! I love it!

PETER: In the shadows—

ANNIE: Like a ghost—

PETER: With just the reflection of the lights hitting her glasses—

ANNIE: Like fireflies!

PETER: And when the aunt goes down the hall to bed there should actually be a bed back there so she can lie down and sleep, not relax with a cup of coffee and *Variety*. And when the little girl comes home, she should come *home*! The dressing room will be made into her bedroom with a dresser and her books and dolls. And when the actors say they are going outside, they should go *outside. Outside the theater!* Onto the street.

(The lights begin to fade.)

PETER: And behind the house there will be dirt, and seeds, so that Vincent can actually farm. No one will ever see—but the actors will see it and feel it and live it—until a world is created—the world of your play!

(End of Scene Two)

ACT ONE

Scene Three

(In the black we hear the thundering music of Beethoven. Lights rise on four actors, in their twenties, sitting in chairs, listening to PETER *with rapt faces as he speaks in a vibrant whisper. In the corner,* ANNIE, *wearing glasses, sits at a small table, piled high with resumes. Occasionally, she starts making notations, but each time she begins, she finds herself listening to* PETER *and puts down her pen.)*

PETER: …and *that's* what I'm looking for and quite honestly, I don't expect to find it. Or rather, I don't expect to find it often. So if and when I do once in a great while find an actor who is willing to give all these things, I feel both honored and humbled. I don't expect any of you to have any real interest in what I've just outlined, all of it is hard, exhausting, *impossible!* —and it's all without pay. I won't be insulted in the least if you get up right now and leave. *(Pause)* No one's left yet, so pray, let me continue. Not only must you be willing and committed and fierce—I like that word, it says what I want it to say—but this work is to be done in a totally unconventional way. My purpose is to break through boundaries, barriers, to reality itself. It is painful and it's something frightening. All of my work is to be done in a totally unconventional way. Now, how does this sound to you so far?

(All the actors speak at once.)

MEG: Sounds good to me.

JOHN: Yeah, boy.

SALLY: Absolutely!

BARNEY: I'll say.

PETER: Now, over here at the table you see Annie—

ANNIE: Hi.

PETER: You all know Annie. She contacted you about this callback. Annie is also a brilliant playwright.

ANNIE: *(Touched)* Thank you, Peter.

PETER: Now, at this precise moment we are on a search to find what will ultimately be a company of twelve actors. I don't know how many we've seen so far, do you know, Annie?

ANNIE: I'm not sure, let me see. *(She rifles through the headshots.)*

PETER: Never mind, I would say it's probably in the hundreds.

ANNIE: No, Peter, I think it's less…just a second, I've got it written down—

PETER: Well, anyway, the point is—

ANNIE: It's here somewhere—

PETER: …the point is a lot of people have sat right where you are—

ANNIE: One hundred sixty-two!

PETER: And so far there is one member.

ANNIE: Sorry, Peter—here it is—one hundred sixty-six, including these four.

PETER: Thank you, Annie.

(BARNEY *raises his hand. He is earnest, eager to please, a generous spirit.*)

PETER: Ah, a question. I'm sorry, your name escapes me…

ANNIE: Barney! Barney McCall.

PETER: Barney McCall. You were here before, Barney? For some reason, I don't remember you.

ANNIE: Actually, Peter. He's a walk-in. He got here too late yesterday so I let him in today.

ACT ONE

PETER: So, Barney, what's your question?

BARNEY: When you say unconventional, do you mean experimental? Or are you talking more of an avant-garde, La Mama sort of thing…I mean, do you mean actual scripts, or maybe not scripts, but the kind of scripts where…well, if you would just…um… clarify… *(Glancing about)* I'm not sure I understand "unconventional". Is anybody else confused…or wondering…or…

PETER: Barney, what's the real question?

BARNEY: I'm not sure. I'm just feeling a little…lost. I've done some improvisational work…if that's what you're talking about.

PETER: I'm talking Grotowski.

BARNEY: Oh! Is he…um…no, that's somebody else…or maybe I am thinking of him, if he's Russian, that is…

PETER: Polish. Grotowski was Polish. Has anyone heard of him?

(The actors are silent.)

PETER: *No one* has heard of Grotowski? Has anyone heard of Laurence Olivier?

(All hands go up.)

PETER: Ahhh. Well, if you take everything that Olivier was and replace it with the opposite, then you have Grotowski! Grotowski's company worked in a *highly* unconventional way. When he did a play about mental illness the audience did not sit separated by an orchestra pit, safe and secure. Oh, no! They were in the asylum, too. They were forced to sit as close to the insanity and to the actors, Barney, as she is to you.

(PETER points to SALLY who has a delicate face and a sweet, fragile presence.)

BARNEY: Wow!

PETER: Does that give you a better idea of "unconventional"?

BARNEY: Yeah!!

PETER: Now, I realize I've talked quite a bit about me, what I'm looking for, what's important to me. Now I want to hear from you. You're John, right?

(PETER *points to a handsome, confident young man.*)

JOHN: That's me.

PETER: And you look like a bright, intelligent young man. What do you think is the best way for us to get re-acquainted?

JOHN: I don't know. I guess we could talk or maybe—audition again?

PETER: No, I don't want to see your masks again. What's that by your foot?

JOHN: Just a resume. I brought an extra—just in case.

PETER: Ahhh, a resume. May I see?

(*As* PETER *studies the resume,* BARNEY *pulls out a noisy package of saltines.* PETER *looks at him until* BARNEY *replaces the crackers in his bag.* PETER *crosses to* ANNIE, *points out something on the resume, and sneers.*)

JOHN: If there's anything more I can tell you—

(PETER *rips the resume in half.*)

JOHN: Hey!

PETER: I hate bullshit.

JOHN: Why'd you—

PETER: What is this "table tennis" shit? What is this "drive a jeep"? Do you think that anybody gives a fuck that you went to N Y U?

JOHN: You asshole! You asked to see it.

ACT ONE

PETER: But you're the one who filled it out. That's what you really think, isn't it? If you can drive a four in the floor, then you can act. Or maybe get a commercial which to you is the same thing. It seems to me, John, that you're just a resume-y sort of guy. Why don't you go? You're in the wrong place. I'm looking for actors.

ANNIE: Peter!

PETER: No, Annie.

JOHN: I'm an actor.

PETER: No, you're not. You've memorized some monologues and according to that *paper* you're the king of all dialects. There are more dialects on your resume than there are countries in the world!

JOHN: Listen, I don't know what your game is but—

PETER: *This is no game!*

JOHN: Then why did you ask me to come back?

PETER: I just said I was looking for gifted actors to form an unconventional acting company. So the real question, my good man, is why are you still here?

JOHN: Fuck you! You're sick! You're a fucking asshole! That's what you are with all your talk about Mister Groteskie or whatever the fuck his name is and I'm going straight to Equity! *(He exits.)*

ANNIE: *(Upset)* Peter? I don't think—wait, John! *John!*

*(*ANNIE *exits.* PETER *crosses towards the other three, takes a chair, and sits.)*

PETER: Now, any more ideas on how we can get re-acquainted?

SALLY: *(Standing)* I think this is sick, too.

PETER: Where are you going?

SALLY: You had no right to talk to him that way. No one should be subjected to that. Who do you think you are, God?

PETER: No, I'm a director. And I'm looking for actors who can act. Are you one of them?

SALLY: No, I couldn't afford the therapy bill. Are the rest of you going to stay for this?

(MEG, *a handsome girl with a strong, magnetic presence starts to rise.* BARNEY *is transfixed.*)

MEG: Come on, let's go.

PETER: *(To* SALLY*)* You didn't answer my question. Are you one of them?

(PETER *stands in* SALLY's *way.*)

PETER: Are you someone who can challenge the rules and play with reality? If you can't, you have no business calling yourself an actor.

SALLY: Please get out of my way.

PETER: Or do things have to be safe with you all the time. Safe and secure and deadly. Oh, acting's fine as long as we never have to be afraid, and reality's fine, too, as long as it never gets too real. That's it, isn't it?

SALLY: I've seen your type before. And I think you're dangerous.

PETER: I am.

SALLY: I'm going to report you to Equity, too.

PETER: Good.

SALLY: Get out of my way.

(SALLY *moves and* PETER *moves with her.*)

SALLY: Get out of my way!!

(*He counters her again.*)

ACT ONE

SALLY: GET OUT OF MY WAY!! *(Weeping)* Somebody help me!

(BARMEY *and* MEG *start toward* SALLY.)

PETER: Get back!

(They get back.)

PETER: I'm talking to Sally right now. So, you're an actress. And I suppose you've had it in your mind that one day you could play Ophelia. Yes, that's what you think. After all, you have that "ethereal quality." But you will never play Ophelia, never. Because Ophelia goes mad and you are deathly afraid of madness, aren't you? You're so afraid of your own that you won't go near it. I would say you've been in therapy a long time. I would say you're in therapy right now. Who's sick, Sally? Hmmm? Who's in danger?

MEG: Son of a bitch!

(MEG *takes a flying leap and tackles* PETER.)

MEG: Leave her the fuck alone! You heard me! *You* get back!

PETER: John! Annie!!

ANNIE: Coming!

(ANNIE *enters with* JOHN.)

PETER: Good work, John.

JOHN: Thanks. *(He crosses the room and takes off his jacket.)*

SALLY: What is going on here?

PETER: This was an improvisation. This is John Hightower. John is already a member. Right, John?

JOHN: That's right.

ANNIE: *(To the girls)* Are you okay?

SALLY: What you just did was *sick*!

PETER: No, that was real. There's a difference. Sally, you're just upset because you were in the dark, that's all. And we're going to talk about it, I want to hear everything you have to say, but since John was in on it, let's start with him. How did it feel, John?

JOHN: Great. I didn't know where you were taking it at first. So I just went with it. What you said was true. I did feel the "prickles". It felt real as hell, but at the same time, I was cool as a cucumber. You know, the cool head and the warm heart?

PETER: I asked John earlier if he would do an improvisation with me and he agreed. I think he did a fine job. I think you did, too, because you believed him, didn't you?

BARNEY: I'll say! That was fantastic. Boy, I was on my way out of here! I thought you were a nutcase for sure!

PETER: *(To* MEG*)* What about you?

MEG: That was so sick I think I'm going to puke!

PETER: But riveting? *(Pause)* Mesmerizing? *(Pause)* Alive?

MEG: Maybe. Also—out of control!

PETER: No, Meg, I was always at the helm. Always. Now, imagine if an audience felt what you just felt. That somebody was actually in danger, that something was actually at stake! That something mattered besides applause.

ANNIE: Can I say something, Peter? I just want to say that, first of all, you were terrific, John—

JOHN: Thanks.

ANNIE: And second of all *(To* SALLY*)* you can play Ophelia, all right! You can also play Kate, she's the oldest sister in my play. Can't you see her, Peter? She's Kate through and through. And as for you, Meg, you

ACT ONE

showed exactly the passion, the rage that we're looking for for Ellen.

PETER: Annie, could I have a word with you?

ANNIE: Sure! What's up?

(They cross away from the others.)

PETER: Stop it.

ANNIE: Stop what?

PETER: Stop doing my job.

ANNIE: I'm sorry. I know I'm getting ahead of myself, but they're so wonderful. They're Ellen and Kate! They even look like sisters.

PETER: Annie—

ANNIE: I know I'm getting ahead of myself, I realize you're the director—

PETER: Annie, let's not have this talk again, okay?

ANNIE: Okay.

(They cross back to the others.)

PETER: Now, let us continue. Sally, you look perturbed. What are you thinking?

SALLY: That I've never been to an audition like this.

PETER: This is true. But there may come a time you'll think this is the only way to work. That is, if you want to work this way. Do you?

BARNEY: I do! Man, that was great!

PETER: Do you, Sally?

SALLY: I don't know.

PETER: Meg?

MEG: I don't know either.

PETER: I'm going out of the room for a few minutes and while I'm gone you can decide if you want to continue this conversation. Forget that a short while ago you all said, "Yes, absolutely, count me in!" People always say yes to the theory, but to live it—ah! There's the rub. And while you're deciding about me, I will be deciding, too, about you. Annie? Would you please come with me?

ANNIE: Certainly.

(ANNIE *and* PETER *exit.*)

MEG: This is weird. This is the weirdest thing that's happened to me today.

BARNEY: I think it's great! I just read *The Fervent Years* and Harold Clurman was right—

SALLY: I think he's insane.

MEG: Me, too.

JOHN: I thought so too in the beginning. But he's right, reality is a taste you acquire and then you can't stand the phony shit anymore. I went to an audition yesterday, and it was almost surreal. Peter made me go on one just to see it for what it is. And I saw. I can't make up anybody's mind for them, but I know I am glad I'm here.

SALLY: He scares me.

JOHN: He scared me, too. You should have seen me! I stormed out when he started doing some of his stunts—and let me tell you, he knows some! But I kept thinking about him and the stuff he said, and I really believe he's on the cutting edge of something. Something big! And I want to be right there with him!

MEG: He reminds me of my high-school chemistry teacher. He was always talking about his formulas and these ideas he'd had that no one has ever had before. He'd get so excited he'd drool, and we didn't know if he was fucking crazy or an Einstein—until he blew up half the school making mouthwash! This ain't for me.

ACT ONE

SALLY: Me either. What would you get out of it anyway? Sounds like a lot of work and worry.

MEG: Yeah, and no money!

BARNEY: Who cares? I would pay for this!

SALLY: I wouldn't! Do you know what I did for eight straight hours today?

MEG: Please. I'm trying to forget.

SALLY: I typed labels. Labels from hospital files. Look at the paper cuts I've got. *(She points to Band-aids on her fingers.)* Here. And look at this one. I had to go inside the folders and search for the names and addresses and then try to find the current one and—

JOHN: Look, we've all got shitty jobs. This is about something that's *not shitty*.

SALLY: Not to me. *(Picking up her bag)* I'm not kidding about the therapy bill, either. I've been through too much lately. No way.

MEG: Which way are you going?

SALLY: Downtown.

MEG: Well, let's go together.

BARNEY: I can't believe the two of you are walking out! Oh, you talk big about being actors—but Peter's right, all you're looking for is applause.

MEG: That's not true. I'm a very dedicated actress. I give a hundred percent when I work on a show. I give more than a hundred percent. I just don't trust him—he's just a little too "fierce".

(PETER and ANNIE enter.)

PETER: That's too bad. Because without trust, nothing is possible.

MEG: Listen, I'm sorry but this just isn't for me. It just isn't. Now, I hope you're going to let me by.

SALLY: Me, too.

PETER: Of course. But would you wait just a minute? I need to talk to Barney first. Would you do that? Just one minute? Okay?

MEG: Okay.

(PETER *crosses to* BARNEY, *who gives him a mock salute.*)

BARNEY: Yes, Herr Directeur?

PETER: Barney, I detest when directors hold out hope to actors and make them wait weeks for a phone that never rings. So I make it a practice to be direct once I have made up my mind. I'm sorry but I just don't feel that this is the best place for you or your talents. I do want to wish you luck. Thanks for coming by—and for all that you've contributed here today.

(PETER *crosses the room, glances back and sees* BARNEY *still staring at him.*)

PETER: Thank you, Barney.

BARNEY: That's it?

PETER: That's it.

BARNEY: Can I ask why?

PETER: I just told you.

BARNEY: No, you didn't.

PETER: At the risk of sounding redundant, I don't think this is where you belong.

BARNEY: Why?

PETER: Barney, this isn't pleasant for me. And it can't be pleasant for you.

BARNEY: But I want to do this! I'm the only one that does!

PETER: I know.

ACT ONE

BARNEY: I would do anything. I just said I would *pay* to do this. I could cut off my arm.

PETER: That would be truly unnecessary.

BARNEY: I want to know. Why did you pick him *(He points to* JOHN.*)* and not me! I can act! I can act up a storm!

PETER: I'm not looking for storms.

BARNEY: I want in.

PETER: Barney, please go.

BARNEY: No. I want to know why. I deserve to be told why. And I'm not leaving until you do.

PETER: All right. *(Pause)* You have no backbone. No depth. No mind of your own. You are an echo, a sponge, a repeater, the ultimate follower. You go where the wind blows, you get excited, you erupt, you float and then you look for the next order, the next leader, the next trend. And that is the truth about you, Barney. I didn't want to work with you and I most certainly wish you would take your things and leave—*now!*

(The others stand to one side and watch as BARNEY *leaves. He is crying.)*

PETER: But I do want to continue talking to you, Sally. And to you, Meg. I'm sorry that Barney's feelings are hurt, I tried to avoid it, but I have a terrible habit of telling the truth when people push me to do so. Barney thought because he was enthusiastic and complimentary that that would mean something. But I don't want followers, tag-alongs. I want unconventional actors who believe in something, and are willing to fight for it. Who have a mind of their own. You are both gifted, and believe me, I have a sense about that. You also have passion and courage. I want you to come back and sit down.

*(*SALLY *and* MEG *appear frozen.)*

PETER: Please.

(They finally look at each other and shrug their shoulders.)

PETER: Please.

(MEG crosses back to her chair and SALLY slowly follows.)

PETER: Annie, please come join us.

(ANNIE and PETER sit close to the others.)

PETER: Now, Sally, let's discuss the improvisation we did together. You were right. It was frightening, it was devious, it was cruel. You saw it for what it was but what made it intolerable for you is the fact that you were in the dark. John was in on it so he feels fine, right, John?

JOHN: I feel great.

PETER: Meg, you were also right when you said there was no trust. There wasn't. A company is created and cemented with trust—and with comradeship and a certain kind of love. As you can see, I don't want people who say "yes" blindly, stupidly, insanely.

SALLY: I feel bad for him. He was a nice guy.

MEG: He's crushed right now.

SALLY: But I'm glad you understand how I felt. That *was* sick.

PETER: Yes, it was.

SALLY: And it was manipulative.

PETER: Yes.

MEG: But it was also—alive.

PETER: Thank you.

MEG: I get so tried of plays where I keep thinking, "they're acting!" I didn't think that once when you were talking to John. *(To SALLY)* Or when he was talking to you.

ACT ONE

SALLY: I know.

MEG: Imagine. If that was the play we were doing and the same realness was there—

SALLY: I know.

MEG: Damn! We'd all win Tonys!!

PETER: Oh, God!

JOHN: Can I say something, Peter?

PETER: By all means.

JOHN: I think we just might have two new members.

ANNIE: And then there were three!

PETER: Not so fast. When I hear remarks about Tony Awards, I get shivers down my spine. This is not about a contest or—Barney, did you forget something?

BARNEY: *(Entering)* I was all the way to Broadway before I caught on.

PETER: Caught on to what?

BARNEY: Hee-hee-hee. I know what this is about. You fooled me. But not for long! No sir. I'm in like Flynn. I'm sticking like a licking. *(He throws down his backpack and sits.)*

PETER: You think I was joking with you?

BARNEY: It took me a while, but I caught on. Is that the way he did you, too, John, when you stormed out? There's a method to the madness!

PETER: What I said to you earlier wasn't a joke. It wasn't a game—and it wasn't an improvisation. Please leave.

BARNEY: *(Angrily)* FUCK YOU!!! *(Grinning)* Pretty good, huh?

PETER: No. John already did that; he did it better.

BARNEY: Okay. How's this? *KISS MY ASS!!!!!!!!* Hee-hee!

(PETER *looks down at his feet.* ANNIE *shakes her head sadly at* BARNEY. *The others look away.*)

BARNEY: You don't all have to talk at the same time. But I wish you would say something. *(Pause)* Anything. *(Pause)* Oh, shit...you weren't kidding, were you? You really don't want me. *(He exits.)*

PETER: Why don't we take a little break. John, if you would escort Sally and Meg over to the diner, Annie and I will join you shortly. This space for the moment is a bit heavily endowed and I think we could all use a change of scenery.

JOHN: Sure. You guys okay?

SALLY: No.

MEG: Help me up.

JOHN: *(Assisting her)* Come on. We'll see you, Peter. Annie.

(*They exit.* ANNIE *gets up and goes to the table and starts packing up her things.*)

PETER: Say it.

ANNIE: Say what?

PETER: What you're thinking.

ANNIE: It's not about me, Peter. I just don't know. There was a better way to tell him. There was a kinder way to say no.

PETER: Annie...I thought you'd learned something in the past few weeks.

ANNIE: Don't change the subject! That was mean. I can't be a party to something that's just pure mean. I can't.

ACT ONE

PETER: Nothing has sunk in. You think I enjoyed rejecting Barney? Causing him pain? I told you it would come to this. I told you back when you asked me to direct your play. I said it will *be impossible because I will ask* the impossible. Didn't I say that?

ANNIE: Maybe.

PETER: It wasn't maybe. It's what I said. Isn't it?

ANNIE: So what if it is?

PETER: Barney is not on the caliber of the others, nor with your play. My standard is high and I will not lower it.

ANNIE: I'm not asking you to lower your standards—

PETER: I won't! Not for you, not for anyone. And the truth is, Annie, I've been having second thoughts all week. I've been feeling a…pressure…to be something I'm not.

ANNIE: What have I said—

PETER: It's not anything you've said. It's just a difference between you and me. I think we're too different.

ANNIE: Don't say that. I want you to direct my play. And these three are perfect for it. So let's just stay with that, okay?

PETER: And then tomorrow I will do something else that will offend you and we'll have this discussion again. No, I don't think it's going to work.

ANNIE: It's working! I watched their faces while you were talking. They didn't want to be but they were swept away. They were excited and caught up—so think of them!

PETER: I want to.

ANNIE: Why don't we go across the street, bring them back, and just—begin. We've been auditioning and auditioning and maybe we just need to start.

PETER: Maybe you're right.

ANNIE: I am right.

PETER: But—

ANNIE: Yes?

PETER: I'm going to need your help, Annie.

ANNIE: You've got it. I've told you before and I'll tell you again, I'll do anything.

PETER: All right, then. Let's start. But with what?

ANNIE: What do you mean?

PETER: We have to give them something to work on—what?

ANNIE: My play.

PETER: Your play's not cast, Annie. It's not going to be cast for a long time. Finding the right little girl, the right elderly woman won't be easy. But I agree, we need to begin something now. I was thinking—if it were two of them, *Miss Julie* would be perfect.

ANNIE: *Miss Julie*?

PETER: Strindberg.

ANNIE: I know who Strindberg is.

PETER: It would be perfect. But there's three of them. But what if there were *two* Miss Julies? What if the girls doubled as Miss Julie? Then they would be just like the sisters in your play, both vying for the attention of Vincent because Vincent in your play is just like Jean in *Miss Julie*!

ANNIE: Have you lost your mind?

ACT ONE

PETER: It could work. It would be a blueprint for your play. It would—

ANNIE: We're not doing *Miss Julie*. We're doing my play. That's what we agreed to do here. *My play!*

PETER: I honestly thought for a moment that you were thinking of someone other than yourself. Annie, this has to be founded on more than just ego.

ANNIE: It is. My money!

PETER: Then take it back. I don't want it. I just wish you would quit lying to me, and to yourself. You don't want to do what's best for these actors, or even for the work itself.

ANNIE: I just don't want to lose any more time.

PETER: Time! Your and your schedules. What you said before was "you can have this room every day!" Every day! You said, "you can work however long it takes!" I'm trying to build a company out of which your play can come to life. You don't care that these actors will have to strip down and expose every last raw nerve they have.

ANNIE: I do care!

PETER: You don't care about anyone but yourself. *(He starts to exit.)*

ANNIE: Where are you going?

PETER: I'm going to go tell the actors to forget it. *(He exits.)*

ANNIE: All right!

(PETER re-enters.)

PETER: All right, what?

ANNIE: All right. We'll do *Miss Julie*. No, I mean it. I swear to God. Go on and work with them. I'll find other things to do while you're busy with them.

PETER: No! I'll be busy with you too. You're in it.

ANNIE: You want me to play Miss Julie, too?

PETER: No. I was hoping you would play Kristen.

ANNIE: The cook?

PETER: You don't have to do it.

ANNIE: No, I told you I will do anything—and I will.

PETER: Thank you. It will be a blueprint for your play. It will make your play great.

(ANNIE *catches his hand and holds it.*)

ANNIE: You have musician's hands. That's what they call hands like yours. Do you realize you've never played the piano for me?

PETER: I told you. I don't play anymore.

ANNIE: That's why I want you to play—just for me. Will you?

PETER: Right now I think we should go across the street. We need to focus on them now and not look too…personal. All right?

ANNIE: Of course.

PETER: I could use a cup of tea.

ANNIE: You also need to eat.

PETER: No, tea's fine. I forgot to cash my check.

ANNIE: So I'll treat.

PETER: No! It doesn't look good in front of the others.

ANNIE: Then here. (*She hands him a bill.*) Pay for it yourself. But you're going to eat.

PETER: All right. But I have something for you. (*He runs up the stairs into his room and returns with a book.*) Here.

ANNIE: Peter, that's your book. I'm not going to take your book.

ACT ONE

PETER: Even after I've inscribed it?

(ANNIE *leafs through the book and finds the inscription.*)

ANNIE: *(Reading)* "To Annie—and new beginnings—Peter."

(ANNIE *looks up at* PETER *and smiles. He gently leads her towards the door. As she exits, he glances back into the rehearsal room and, with a look of utter satisfaction, he turns out the lights.*)

END OF ACT ONE

ACT TWO

Scene One

(In the dark we hear voices in the middle of a rehearsal warm-up. The voices overlap and grow louder and louder.)

(Lights rise on SALLY *and* JOHN *stretched out on the floor.* MEG *is standing, bent over at the waist, dangling her arms to the floor.)*

JOHN: *(Like a tugboat)* OOOWWWW, OOOOWWWWWW!

SALLY: *(Like a dog)* Yip, yip, yip, yip, yip!

MEG: *(Like an exaggerated yawning sound)* Ohhh, ohhh, ohhh.

*(*PETER *is crossing about the room, focusing spotlights and encouraging the actors to relax. He pauses near* MEG *and begins whispering in her ear just as* ANNIE, *loaded down with shopping bags, rushes in. Glancing quickly at* PETER *and* MEG, ANNIE *puts the bags in a corner, removes her coat, turns on an electric skillet sitting near the wall, and joins the others on the floor.)*

PETER: That's right. Relax. Begin to let go. Let it go. Let it go. That's right, let it go.

*(*JOHN's *hand is stretched out on the floor, touching* MEG's. PETER *crosses quickly and separates them.)*

PETER: Keep your hands to yourself.

ALL: Ooooohhhhh…eeeee…ooooowwwwww.

PETER: You're relaxed now. Your torsos should be melting into the floor. Your arms and legs are just hanging…hanging…your fingers have melted.

ALL: Ahhhhhh…ha, ha, ha!

PETER: Now, just lay there for a minute and feel totally relaxed. And now slowly, slowly, slowly, begin to sit up.

(ANNIE *pops into a sitting position.*)

PETER: *Slowly.*

(ANNIE *returns to the floor.*)

PETER: And when you're ready, I want you to open your eyes and begin an improvisation based on *Miss Julie.*

(*The actors slowly open their eyes, blink, stretch, and yawn.* ANNIE *still looks self-conscious.* PETER *has positioned small spotlights to criss-cross the playing area. He now turns out the overhead lights, giving the room a haunted, mysterious glow.*)

PETER: Begin an improv based on *Miss Julie.*

(PETER *retires to a corner with a notebook. He watches the others from time to time and then writes obsessively, sometimes ripping the paper with his intensity.* SALLY *and* MEG *rise and go into separate areas, putting on various pieces of costume—a frock coat for* MEG, *a long fancy robe for* SALLY. MEG *preens in front of an imaginary mirror;* SALLY *dances about, eyes closed.* JOHN *puts on an apron, then begins shining a pair of black riding boots.* ANNIE *looks bewildered. After tying a red scarf, peasant-style, on her head, she snaps open a red apron and ties that on, too. She turns on an electric skillet, then rifles through her shopping bags, clattering dishes and emptying a package of hamburger meat into a pan. She sits pounding the meat with a metal utensil.)*

ACT TWO

PETER: *Miss Julie* is not a play about food.

ANNIE: *(Freezing)* Oh.

(ANNIE *crouches on the floor, unsure of what to do next. She lifts the lid to the electric skillet and pours water into it from her Evian bottle. A great cloud of steam fills the air which she tries to disperse with the skillet lid.*)

PETER: This is *not* a play about food.

(ANNIE *replaces the lid and cowers, waiting.*)

SALLY: *(Singing:)* La-de-da, la-la-la.

MEG: *(Singing as she dances)* La-la-la-la-la.

PETER: That's right. Become the characters. It's about being.

ANNIE: Oh, Jean! Jean? Supper's ready! *(Crossing to him)* There you are! Come on in! I've got your favorite dinner ready—

PETER: THIS IS NOT A PLAY ABOUT FOOD!

ANNIE: Sorry.

PETER: Do not acknowledge me. I am not here.

ANNIE: Okay.

(PETER *crosses to the skillet and rips the plug out of the socket.*)

PETER: Your job is to *be*.

ANNIE: Fine.

(ANNIE *crosses into a far corner and* MEG *and* SALLY *move towards* JOHN.)

MEG: *(Laughing)* Oh, Jean!

SALLY: *(Vying for his attention)* Jean…oh, Jean…

(MEG *throws her long scarf around* JOHN's *neck.* SALLY *quickly unwinds it and throws it back onto* MEG.)

PETER: That's right, *be* the characters. Let your actions be in line with the play. Good. Very good.

ANNIE: *(Nervous, but determined)* Jean? Why don't you come on in for dinner?

PETER: God.

ANNIE: All right. Can we stop for a minute, Peter?

PETER: No.

ANNIE: But I'm doing this all wrong. I thought since Kristen is the cook that I would cook but evidently that's not it. I don't know what is.

PETER: Don't talk.

ANNIE: But I don't know—

PETER: Annie, this is not a play about the cook! If you must know, Kristen sleeps throughout the whole play.

ANNIE: So?

PETER: So, sleep.

(Enraged, ANNIE *goes to a chair and sits. She stretches out and closes her eyes as if in sleep.* JOHN *crosses and sits next to her.)*

JOHN: You should have seen her dancing. She was wild!

ANNIE: *(Almost hissing)* Who?

JOHN: Miss Julie! You should have seen her.

SALLY: *(Running to* JOHN*)* What a charming escort, running away from his partner! Come dance with me again!

*(*JOHN *crosses back to the boots and resumes his polishing.)*

SALLY: You are a superb dancer. Put the boots down.

JOHN: No, I have work to do. I never agreed to be your playmate, and never will. It's beneath me.

(At a loss, SALLY *glances at* PETER.*)*

ACT TWO

PETER: Don't look at me! Stay with your objective, Sally. Stay with it.

SALLY: Jean! Come outside—and pick lilacs for me!

JOHN: Absolutely not. Someone might see us.

SALLY: And think I've fallen in love with a servant?

JOHN: Never step down, Miss Julie. People will say you fell.

PETER: Meg, find your way into this.

MEG: Jean is not going outside with you. He is going to drink to my health. Aren't you, Jean? *(She holds out a bottle of water.)* You must, Jean! I order you to.

JOHN: Then I obey. *(Taking the bottle)* Miss Julie, you can't drink beer.

MEG: I prefer beer to wine!

JOHN: You are stepping down. Don't you know it's dangerous to play with fire?

MEG: Not for me—I'm insured.

JOHN: No, you're not. But even if you were, there's combustible material close by. *(He takes the bottle from her and gets down on one knee. In mock-romantic fashion)* Skäol to my mistress!

MEG: Bravo! Now kiss my boot to finish it properly.

(As he kisses her shoe)

MEG: Perfect! *(She yanks him up by his hair.)* You should have been an actor! *(She gives him a quick slap on the face as she turns away.)*

(SALLY crosses to JOHN and MEG. She is carrying a candelabra, with all the candles lit.)

PETER: Careful with the candles. Sally, be careful.

SALLY: NO! I am Miss Julie!!!! I can do anything! *(She kisses MEG while looking teasingly at JOHN. She laughs and crosses to* ANNIE.) She certainly can sleep! She probably snores, too. Wake up, Cook! Wake up! I'm hungry!

ANNIE: *(Mouthing to* PETER*)* What is she doing?

PETER: Very good, Sally.

MEG: I'm hungry, too. Wake up, Cook, and feed me first!

JOHN: Can't you see she's sleeping?

MEG: What do I care if she's sleeping? The night is magic and I can do and be anything I please. I am Miss Julie!

JOHN: Kristen— Wake up!

ANNIE: Lord!

PETER: Stay in character.

ANNIE: I am in character. I'm the damn maid.

PETER: Do not acknowledge me.

ANNIE: Damned if I do and damned if I don't.

PETER: All right. The three of you please continue your improv in the hallway.

SALLY: *(To* JOHN*)* Catch me if you can!

JOHN: Miss Julie! You are wild tonight!

(They exit on the run, laughing.)

PETER: What is this about, Annie? What are you trying to do?

ANNIE: You tell me! You said come prepared to be your character. Well, I'm not an actress but I hauled that shit sixty city blocks. I've got pancake mix and apples and hamburger meat and an Entenmann's cake and now that's wrong…well, fuck me!

PETER: Annie, this is not a play about—

ANNIE: Shut up! I know! I have tried everything. Day after day. I don't know what I'm doing. You say be

Kristen—she doesn't do anything except cook. Cook and sleep!

PETER: Yes, she does.

ANNIE: What?

PETER: *(Gently)* She accepts, Annie. She accepts. Accepting can be an action.

ANNIE: I have tried so hard.

PETER: That's the problem. All you're doing is struggling. Try to accept—everything. Miss Julie giving you orders. Jean talking about her to you, your station in life, your sex. Learn to accept.

ANNIE: *(Crying)* It's not fair. They get to wear fun clothes and be pretty! What am I saying? Why am I trying to act? I'm not an actor. And why am I playing a maid? There's no maid in my play for Crissakes! Screw the maid!

PETER: Is this the point of our rehearsal? Is this what we've come to—whether or not you're the center of attention?

ANNIE: How dare you talk to me that way! How dare you!

PETER: Your selfishness is astounding!

ANNIE: *My selfishness? Excuse me???* Who gets here early and sweeps up and makes the coffee and pays for the space and lets those assholes in and—

PETER: Yes, your selfishness!! You are so caught up with yourself you can't see the miracle that's happening before your very eyes. They are becoming the people in your play, Annie. Just now, Meg was Ellen. And Sally was Kate. And John is so close. Have you forgotten why we're here? Yes, you lock up and sweep. Yes, I stay up half the night planning exercises and improvs because you have your job and I have mine. We made an agreement but we can cancel it at any time. Shall we?

ANNIE: I don't know what I want. I'm tired. I feel—stupid. I feel like the maid.

PETER: Kristen is not a maid—she's a cook. And her purpose is to support and accept. Can you play this role or not?

ANNIE: Yes. Yes, I can. You know I want this more than anything. Peter, I care so much! You know that. Last night when I got home I wrote two new monologues for the scene where Vincent traps Kate on the porch. I'd like to go over it with you—tonight, after rehearsal. I think I've nailed it, Peter. I think it's there. We'll order in Chinese, okay?

PETER: All right, we'll see. Right now, I need to see what the others are up to. *(He starts to exit.)*

ANNIE: In fact, I got so inspired, I bought you a present, see? *(She opens the piano bench and pulls out sheet music, adorned with a big green ribbon.)* It's *Moonlight Sonata*. I love that piece. I thought maybe you could play it for me—later.

PETER: *(Replacing the sheet music in the piano bench)* Annie, this is what worries me about you. This is what concerns me.

ANNIE: What worries you? That I bought you a present? That I'd like to work on my play? What?

PETER: That you're already living at midnight eating Chinese food while I play you sonatas. Annie! We're here now. Here. In this moment. In this room. If we live this moment totally, chances are midnight will be totally lived, too. Can you understand that?

ANNIE: All right. As long as we can have some time to work on the play. And relax a little and—

ACT TWO

PETER: *Stay in the moment, Annie. Don't leave it again!!* You are Kristen.

ANNIE: Right!

PETER: Okay?

ANNIE: Okay!

PETER: So please put the food away, as Kristen, and prepare yourself for?

ANNIE: Sleep!!! I imagine.

(ANNIE *goes to her corner and starts to pack up an Entenmann's cake.* PETER *goes into the hallway.*)

PETER: John? Meg? Sally? Let's continue, please! John! Meg—

MEG: *(Flying through the door)* I'm not coming because you called, I'm coming because I'm hungry!

(MEG *runs to* ANNIE *and takes a huge chunk of the cake and breaks it in half. She bites into one half and dances around* PETER, *laughing.*)

PETER: All right, Meg. Sit.

MEG: No!

PETER: Yes.

MEG: I said—*(Pushing the cake into his face)*—NO!!!!!

(MEG *giggles and backs away from* PETER. *He lunges forward to grab her, misses, and chases her first into one corner, then another. Finally, he manages to tackle her and he half-carries her into the chair sitting down center. She is screaming in excitement as* JOHN *enters.*)

JOHN: Peter? What's going on?

PETER: Where's Sally?

JOHN: I locked her out on the roof.

PETER: Well, go get her!

JOHN: *(Running out)* Sally!!!!

MEG: I can do anything I want! I am Miss Julie!

PETER: We'll see about that. Annie, hand me that rope over there. In the box!

(ANNIE *brings him a piece of rope.* JOHN *and* SALLY *enter, laughing wildly.*)

PETER: John, hold her arms back there. Sally, help him.

MEG: *(Almost hysterical)* I'm not scared of you or you or you. I am MISSSS JULIEEEEEEEEEEEE!!!

SALLY: No, you're not. I am! Aren't I, Jean?

JOHN: Are we still going, Peter?

PETER: No, I want you to stop. This is something new.

JOHN: Sure. What are we doing with this? Tying her up?

MEG: Tie me up—if you dare!

PETER: Tie her up. Sally, grab that piece of cloth from that box and gag her with it.

SALLY: Is this part of the improv—or what?

PETER: Just get the cloth.

(MEG *is chanting "I am Miss Julie" at high pitch until* SALLY *shoves the cloth into her mouth, cutting her off in mid-sentence.* SALLY *laughs and claps her hands in delight.*)

PETER: There. Now, Meg, how do you feel?

(MEG *kicks one of her legs in the air. We can see that she is still laughing.*)

PETER: Look at her. This is wonderful. She is becoming her character.

JOHN: Peter, we were on the roof. I know you didn't see, but we were real close to the edge, weren't we, Sally?

SALLY: Yes, I lost one of my combs. We were pretty intense!

ACT TWO

PETER: Well, that I didn't see, but don't worry, you'll be part of the exercise. We will focus on Meg, but it will concern us all. Meg, I want you to listen to me very closely. Don't cross your eyes at me. This is serious! And don't wink at me, either. We are going to do an exercise that I think will strengthen your Miss Julie. Right now, she is all high spirits and rebellion but she must experience more than that for Annie's play. Much more. We are going to try to break your spirit, okay?

(MEG *pounds one foot on the floor, like a horse. She moves her head up and down like a horse, too.*)

PETER: This is called the Terror Exercise. If at any time you want us to stop, all you have to do is drop your head on your chest. Like this. *(He shows her.)* Okay? We will stop immediately. Your spirit will be broken, you will lose, but we will stop. Is that understood? Nod your head if you agree to the terms.

(MEG *nods her head like a wind-up toy, over and over and over.*)

PETER: John, get the scarf in the box under the stairs— for a blindfold.

JOHN: Here you go.

PETER: Put it on her.

JOHN: Sure.

PETER: Make it tight.

JOHN: It's pretty tight. Is that too tight, Meg?

(She nods vigorously.)

PETER: I said make it tight!

JOHN: She said it was too tight.

PETER: *THIS IS A TERROR EXERCISE!!* You are the terrorist. She is the hostage. You don't ask the hostage if it's too tight! You don't ask the private if his pack is too heavy. *YOU LIVE IT!!*

JOHN: I'll live anything you want. But I'm not going to hurt Meg.

PETER: Annie, help Sally untie Meg. I need to talk to John.

(ANNIE *and* SALLY *cross to* MEG *and remove her blindfold and gag.*)

PETER: Come here, John.

JOHN: What?

PETER: You are breaking one of the cardinal rules of rehearsal and I won't tolerate it.

JOHN: What do you mean?

PETER: You've got a crush on Meg.

JOHN: I do not!

PETER: You've got a crush on Meg and that's going to kill everything. It will blunt your concentration, your willingness to go the distance—

JOHN: I don't know what you're talking about.

PETER: I've watched you for the past week watching her. Last night you took her home.

JOHN: So what? I've taken Sally home too. I've taken them both home. I'm not seeing Meg.

PETER: But you'd like to, wouldn't you? (*Pause*) Yes, you would. And that creates a wedge between the three of you. And it causes damage.

(PETER *crosses over to the women.*)

PETER: Sally, Meg, we have a problem.

JOHN: Peter!

PETER: No, John, I believe in being honest. I'm afraid John cares for one of you more than the other. He finds one of you more attractive. He doesn't think that that's a problem. How do you feel?

ACT TWO   45

MEG: Well, of course, he loves me!

SALLY: Are we still improv-ing?

PETER: No.

SALLY: Eeek. Then I'd rather not know.

PETER: No, we need to address it and move past it. We can't work together if there is intrigue and secrets. And the only way to move past this, John, is to face it. Are you willing to do an exercise?

JOHN: What kind of exercise?

PETER: One that will prove to the others that you care about this work as deeply as they do. They can't go mountain climbing with someone they're not sure of.

JOHN: They can be sure of me.

PETER: Then you'll sit in the chair?

JOHN: Sure. Why not?

(JOHN *sits.* PETER *crosses to light switch and dims the lights.*)

PETER: Close your eyes. Take a deep breath. All right, John, you're no longer John, you're Jean and you're thinking of Miss Julie. Breathe. You are dreaming of her. You can see her right now in your mind's eye. Do you see her?

(JOHN *nods.*)

PETER: She's beautiful, isn't she? Beautiful eyes. Beautiful hair. She is dancing before you. She's laughing. You want to touch her, don't you? Relax, you're no longer John—you're Jean. Relax and breathe. Let yourself go deep into your imagination. I'm going to ask Miss Julie to caress your face. Is that all right with you?

(JOHN *nods again, his mouth ajar, limbs sprawled.* PETER *motions* MEG *to* JOHN. *He indicates she should touch his face, which she does gingerly.* JOHN *sighs and trembles.*)

PETER: You are fascinated by her, aren't you, Jean? Say something to him, Miss Julie.

MEG: Hello, Jean.

JOHN: Hello.

PETER: Now, I'm going to have Miss Julie kiss you. Is that all right, Jean?

JOHN: Yes. Yes!

PETER: In fact, we're going to leave you alone with Miss Julie. I expect you to *be* your character. You may not get out of the chair. But you are to respond to her as Jean—is that understood?

JOHN: *Yeah. Yes. Yes!*

(PETER, ANNIE, *and* MEG *move towards the door.* SALLY *glances at* PETER *for her cue, then bends down and kisses* JOHN, *slowly at first, then with greater and greater intensity.* JOHN *begins to moan.* PETER *whispers to* ANNIE *at the door, then starts back towards* JOHN *and* SALLY *on tip-toe.* ANNIE *slams the door with a loud bang, during which* PETER *moves quickly next to* SALLY. *He indicates for* SALLY *to move away and now it is* PETER, *not* SALLY, *kissing* JOHN *on his neck and chest. He runs his hands over his chest and down his legs and then up the inside of his thigh as* JOHN *moans in excitement.*)

PETER: *(To* ANNIE*)* And—*LIGHTS!*

(JOHN *opens his eyes and jumps up, knocking his chair across the room. The women burst into laughter.*)

JOHN: Christ! What the hell are you doing, man? What is going on?

PETER: Proving a point.

JOHN: *Jesus Christ!*

ACT TWO

PETER: The point being—it is not how you feel at any particular moment in your narrow little self—it's about your responsibility as an actor to do your job! It's about being willing to go the distance. Now sit down, John. The exercise is not over.

JOHN: I think it is!

PETER: Sit down or walk out now and never come back.

JOHN: You're fucked, man.

PETER: No, I'm thorough. Either sit down or leave.

JOHN: Fine.

MEG: John!

SALLY: John!

JOHN: What?

MEG: Don't leave. Please.

SALLY: Please!

ANNIE: John, he knows what he's doing.

JOHN: Oh, really? I thought he was an arrogant asshole!

PETER: What's that?

ANNIE: All right, I was mad and I said it. But I was wrong. *(To JOHN)* John, don't lose the reason we're here. We're on the way to something in this room. You can feel it, I know you can.

PETER: Leave him alone. He has to make up his own mind. Decide, John. Decide if you're with us or against us. Decide one or the other, but do it now.

JOHN: *(Sitting)* Shit.

PETER: Now close your eyes. Someone is going to kiss you. It could be Sally or Meg. Or Annie. Or me. Let go. Relax.

JOHN: Shit.

PETER: Relax!

(PETER *nods at* MEG. *She steps forward and kisses* JOHN *lightly.*)

PETER: All right, Jean. Open your eyes. Now kiss her.

(JOHN *does.*)

PETER: Now kiss that Miss Julie.

(MEG *continues to kiss* JOHN.)

PETER: I said, kiss *that* Miss Julie!

(JOHN *does.*)

PETER: Now kiss Kristen, the cook.

(JOHN *does.*)

PETER: Now, give me a—

(PETER *is bent over in front of* JOHN *and dangerously close to* JOHN's *mouth. He suddenly straightens and holds out his arms.*)

PETER: —hug!

(JOHN *laughs almost hysterically in relief and quickly stands to give* PETER *a hug.* PETER *slaps him on the back and* JOHN *reciprocates.*)

PETER: Did you learn something? Huh? Did you?

JOHN: Yeah. I guess so!

PETER: Good. That's why we're here. To learn. Right?

JOHN: Yeah.

PETER: And to be there for everybody, right?

JOHN: Yes.

PETER: So if I ask you to tie up—or kiss—Meg or Sally do you see that it will be all right? That I won't let any harm come to them? Can you trust me?

JOHN: *(Softly)* Yes. *(Then, louder)* Yes.

PETER: *(Staring at him steadily for a long moment)* Can you?

ACT TWO

JOHN: Yes, Peter, I can. I trust you.

PETER: Good. And now they need to trust you. So I want you to take them someplace. I don't care where. Lincoln Center. Your apartment. A church. But you are to be with them both. Can you do that?

JOHN: Oh, yes!

PETER: It's about trust and love, John, not a selfish crush.

JOHN: Okay, Peter.

PETER: I want you to leave, all three of you, and come back in two hours.

SALLY: Come with me, Jean! And I will kiss you again. Take me down to the river.

MEG: No, he's going to ride with me in the park. Aren't you, Jean?

JOHN: *(Laughing)* Oh my God! How am I going to do this?

PETER: As your character. The work is still going on. All of you are to stay in character.

JOHN: Whatever you say!

(The girls giggling and calling out "Jean!" exit with JOHN *one step behind.* PETER *follows them into the hallway.)*

PETER: Take care of both of them! Spend time with both of them! Pay attention to both of them—equally!!

*(*PETER *re-enters, laughing. He sees* ANNIE *across the room and freezes.)*

PETER: What?

ANNIE: *(In tears)* That was Scene Five, wasn't it? When Aunt Rose forces Vincent into the chair. He's so afraid of her and so defiant, and so in love with Kate. But he sits there and endures and that's what you got him to do. Oh, Peter. He was *there*! He was Vincent.

PETER: Thank you.

ANNIE: I'm crying because I can see it.

(ANNIE *runs across the room, leaps up on a chair, and jumps into his arms, straddling him with her legs. Smiling, but slightly shocked,* PETER *holds her as she caresses his face.)*

ANNIE: You're amazing, aren't you? You are! And I've been whining and irritable. But now, it's full steam ahead. I see where you're taking it. What can I do for you? What can I give you?

PETER: If you really must know, I would like to ask a favor.

ANNIE: Yes?

(PETER *whispers in* ANNIE's *ear. She slaps him playfully.)*

ANNIE: How dare you!

PETER: Well, you asked.

ANNIE: No, I will not kiss your boots.

PETER: I didn't say kiss.

ANNIE: Yes, you did.

PETER: No, I didn't. I said *lick* my boots.

ANNIE: Asshole!

PETER: Say you will. Say it!

ANNIE: No! You'll have to tie *me* in a chair!

PETER: I will! You know I will! *(Then, intensely)* Annie?

ANNIE: Yes?

PETER: Say "yes".

(PETER *is kneeling on the floor, still holding* ANNIE *in his arms.)*

ANNIE: To what?

PETER: Just say it.

ACT TWO 51

ANNIE: Why?

PETER: Just say it.

ANNIE: Yes.

PETER: Say it again.

ANNIE: Yes.

PETER: Again.

ANNIE: Yes.

PETER: Keep saying it.

ANNIE: Yes…yes…yes…

(The lights fade on ANNIE *and* PETER *as they embrace.)*

(End of Scene One)

Scene Two

(A few hours later. Lights rise in the rehearsal room. PETER, ANNIE, JOHN, *and* SALLY *sit about, waiting.* ANNIE *and* PETER *look relaxed, peaceful but* SALLY *and* JOHN *are tense, expectant.)*

JOHN: I'm going to try again.

PETER: John, sit.

JOHN: She might have called my machine. Or she might have gone home.

PETER: You just called. Sit.

JOHN: She could be lying in a gutter somewhere.

SALLY: She was dancing around that pole on the subway like it was a Maypole. Remember the man with no teeth trying to dance with her.

JOHN: I'm going to call.

PETER: I said, sit.

JOHN: Peter, something could have happened to her.

PETER: Something did happen to her. She's become Miss Julie.

SALLY: But don't you care about her? What if she does get hurt? She's out of her mind right now.

PETER: Just because she didn't get off the train with you?

SALLY: Oh, she got off! Long enough to run back on. I hurt my arm trying to keep the door open. It closed on me—look!

JOHN: She wouldn't get off.

SALLY: She waved to us like she'd just won the lottery. Running up and down the car! Waving and dancing! I'm afraid for her.

PETER: She's the only one of you with any sense. She's the only one who obeyed my instructions.

SALLY: What?

PETER: She flaunted you! Just the way she's flaunting me and the rules of our rehearsal. I said be back in two hours and she's saying *"No!"* just as Miss Julie says no. She has become Miss Julie.

ANNIE: Still and all, people need to do as they're told. Regardless of the reasons why—

JOHN: *(To* PETER*)* I think you're the one that's insane. What does it matter who she's become if she's gotten herself killed?

PETER: People die every day, John. They die in wars. They die in accidents. WHERE IS IT WRITTEN THAT ACTORS ARE TO BE TREATED LIKE SPUN GLASS? I'm not asking you just to cavort around like children, I'm demanding that you experience something. Do people fawn over recruits in boot camp? Do they? Well, this is your training.

ACT TWO

ANNIE: I know she's fine. Meg is strong, strong as steel. This is something Ellen would do. *(To* PETER*)* In fact, this is very much like Ellen…

(PETER *acknowledges this with an intimate look. They laugh together.* JOHN *crosses to the door, opens it, and yells so loudly the others jump.)*

JOHN: *MEGGGGGGGGGGG!!!!!!!!!!!!*

(JOHN *comes back into room. From the hallway we hear)*

MEG: Yes?

(MEG *enters. She has placed flowers in her hair. She looks wild, manic, but also in total command.)*

MEG: You called?

*(*ANNIE, JOHN, *and* SALLY *go to her. They all speak at once.)*

JOHN: Jesus Christ, Meg, you scared us to death.

SALLY: Why did you stay on the train? Are you nuts?

ANNIE: I knew she was fine, didn't I say so?

PETER: Welcome back, Meg.

MEG: Hello, Peter.

PETER: We've been waiting for you.

MEG: *(Smiling)* I know.

PETER: Why did you make us wait?

MEG: Because I *am* Miss Julie.

PETER: *(To* SALLY*)* Ahhh!

(SALLY *crosses away with a look of disgust.)*

PETER: And, as Miss Julie, are you ready now to do the Terror Exercise?

MEG: Oh, yes.

JOHN: *(Still angry)* Meg, you really had us worried!

PETER: Meg, please tell John you're all right.

MEG: I'm all right, John. Come on, if I can do this, you can do this. Unless, of course, you can't.

(MEG *sits and looks up at* PETER *with a look of absolute power.*)

MEG: Go on, try and scare me.

PETER: This is the moment we have all been waiting for. This is what our work has brought us to, so I need all of you to do your part.

(PETER *has gone under the stairs and pulled out a stainless steel toolbox. He unlocks the box and takes out a pair of cloth handcuffs—the type found in an S & M store.*)

PETER: John, restrain her.

(PETER *tosses the handcuffs to* JOHN *who holds them close to* MEG's *ear and opens them with loud rips.* PETER *takes what looks to be a horse's bit from the box. It is made of black leather and metal.*)

PETER: Sally, use this as a gag.

(SALLY, *giggling self-consciously, crosses to* MEG *and manages to insert the bit in her mouth, tying the leather straps behind her head.*)

PETER: There's a box in my room, Meg. I prepared it just for you. A box. What's in the box? A famous author once said, "Come, drag your chair to a precipice and I'll tell you a tale." Would you like to drag your chair to a precipice while I tell you a tale?

(MEG *shrugs her shoulders as if to say, "why not".*)

PETER: Good. I was hoping you would say yes. That was a yes, wasn't it? Please nod your head if that was a yes.

(MEG *nods her head.*)

PETER: Now remember, all you have to do is drop your head and we will stop. Your spirit will be broken and

ACT TWO

you will lose but we will stop. Nod your head if you agree to those terms.

(MEG *nods again.*)

PETER: Sally, go to my room, look under my bed, and bring down the box.

(SALLY *exits.*)

PETER: But there are such things as sadists, aren't there? Maybe I'm a sadist, too. Remember the first day when I said I was in control? What if I lied, Meg? What if we start playing a game and I enjoy it so much I don't want to stop?

(PETER *is blindfolding* MEG *with a black scarf. He ties it very, very tight.* SALLY *descends the stairs from* PETER's *room carrying a large wooden box, with air holes cut into the sides. There is a scratching noise inside the box.*)

SALLY: What's in here, Peter? Something's in here.

PETER: Just bring it here.

SALLY: Good God, something's in here. I can't.

(SALLY *crosses down center and puts the box on the floor. She backs away nervously.*)

PETER: ANNIE! Pick up the box!

(ANNIE *crosses over, bends down, and picks up the box. We hear the scratching sound again.*)

ANNIE: There is something in here.

PETER: Bring it over here.

(ANNIE *crosses up to* PETER *and* MEG.)

ANNIE: Here, Peter.

PETER: No, I want you to hold it. I want you to hold it up next to Meg's head. I want Meg to try to guess what's in the box!

ANNIE: Okay, sure. It's okay, Meg—

PETER: *Without talking!*

(*As* ANNIE *holds the box up to* MEG's *head,* MEG *tries to back away. She writhes in the chair, moaning, as the box comes closer and closer.*)

PETER: Hold it closer.

ANNIE: Dear God, there's something in there!

PETER: Give it to me.

(PETER *yanks it from* ANNIE *and bangs it down on a small table nearby.*)

PETER: Now let's see what's in the box!

(MEG *is frenzied now, moving from side to side in her chair, her chair scraping the floor.*)

PETER: I'm opening the box, Meg.

(PETER *slides open the lid of the box and just as quickly slams it shut. The actors cry out in alarm.* PETER *once again opens the box and after grappling about lifts a large writhing snake high in the air. He throws it back into the box as the actors gasp.* MEG's *body freezes.*)

PETER: Meg, you once told me you wanted to play Medusa. Well—(*He holds up the box*) here's your chance!

(PETER *upends the box and dozens of snakes fall out and onto* MEG, *landing in her hair, her lap, on the floor. The actors, realizing the snakes are fake, jump to* MEG's *rescue.* MEG *has collapsed and her body is heaving with repetitive spasms.* JOHN *unties her gag and flings it across the room while* ANNIE *tries to remove the blindfold.*)

JOHN: This is bullshit, Peter! Bullshit! Somebody get a towel.

(SALLY *runs from the room.*)

JOHN: Meg, are you all right? Oh my God, she's puking. She's puking all over.

ANNIE: It's okay, Meg, it's okay!

ACT TWO 57

PETER: Good work, Meg!

(MEG *smiles at* PETER.)

MEG: Thank you.

(SALLY *re-enters with a fistful of paper towels.*)

SALLY: Here, Meg! Here!

PETER: There's nothing to clean up, Sally.

SALLY: What do you mean?

PETER: Tell her, Meg.

MEG: *(Smiling)* There's nothing to clean up because I didn't get sick.

JOHN: Jesus.

MEG: *(Laughing merrily)* Because I was acting, John! Isn't that what we're supposed to be doing here—acting?

JOHN: Oh, my God.

(PETER *picks* MEG *up and whirls her around.*)

PETER: This is what I mean when I say commitment. This is what I mean when I say fierce!

(*The other actors begin to laugh.* JOHN *tosses a handful of snakes onto* SALLY *and* ANNIE. *They laugh harder, starting to hug one another until finally all five have formed a small huddle, arms around each other in one big embrace.*)

PETER: I said no one would come to harm. I said you could trust me and you can. You were many things tonight, John. Strong and concerned and that's what this is about. It's about love and concern—

BARNEY: Is that what this is all about? Is that it?

(PETER *looks up and sees* BARNEY *standing in the lighting booth. All of them turn and stare.* BARNEY *looks wrinkled, in need of sleep and a little crazed.*)

PETER: How did you get in here?

BARNEY: Is it really about love?

MEG: Oh my God, it's that guy!

JOHN: Not him!

SALLY: What's he doing?

PETER: What's his name, Annie?

ANNIE: Barney!

PETER: Oh yes, good old Barney. *(Louder)* Barney, come on down. Come on. Annie, go out in the hall and call the police. Barney is going to jail.

ANNIE: *(At the door)* It won't open.

PETER: Why not?

ANNIE: It's chained.

JOHN: *(Crossing to her)* Let me see.

BARNEY: I'm glad to know it's about love, because it sure isn't about talent. All they do is cry and complain and get scared. So why did you pick them? I'm not leaving until you explain it to me.

MEG: Peter, get us out of here.

SALLY: Get him to open the door!

PETER: All right, Barney. The joke's gone on far enough. Come down and unchain the door and let us out.

BARNEY: No.

ANNIE: Barney, I know you're upset and frankly, I don't blame you. Why don't you come down here and talk to us and I know we can straighten everything out.

BARNEY: *(Making a Nazi salute through the window)* Nein, fraulein!

(The actors converge in a corner, whispering excitedly. PETER tries to calm them, also in whispers.)

BARNEY: What are you saying? Don't keep on keeping me out.

ACT TWO

PETER: I'm sorry. I was just telling them that I really have to hand it to you, Barney. You've really shown me something.

BARNEY: What? That I got in?

PETER: No, I'm talking about what's really going on. I think it's rather…brilliant.

BARNEY: You're just flattering me.

PETER: No, it's the truth. This is the most interesting thing that's happened all night. Haven't you been here all night?

BARNEY: No.

PETER: Yes, you have.

BARNEY: No! I've been here all week. Now *that's* brilliant!

PETER: You are smart, Barney.

BARNEY: I am. I've got you locked in tighter than a drum.

PETER: So we're your hostages. What's the ransom, Barney? What do you want?

BARNEY: I want in.

PETER: I believe you do.

BARNEY: I want in so I can do one of your famous exercises. I've watched enough of them. It's time for me to show you what I can do.

PETER: Come on down, then, and show us.

BARNEY: Not them. It has nothing to do with them. This is between me and you.

MEG: Just get him to open the door!

ANNIE: Please, Peter.

PETER: Let me handle this. I think I know an exercise that you and I can play. But if I win you have to unchain the door and let us out. Is that a deal?

BARNEY: Sure.

PETER: I think this fits the occasion rather well. It's called Master/Slave. Have you heard of it?

BARNEY: I trust one of us is the master and the other is the slave?

PETER: Correct. And whoever is the slave has to obey. The slave must do everything the master orders—

BARNEY: So how does the slave win?

PETER: By obeying too well. By going too far. By outdoing the master.

BARNEY: But says *who*? Who says who wins?

PETER: Oh, one knows.

BARNEY: No, let them pick the winner.

PETER: Well, that's hardly fair. After all, I'm their director. They work with me.

BARNEY: Yes, and you're screwing one of them, aren't you? But which one? That's the question. Is it Meg? Or Sally? Or Annie? Or *Jean*?

PETER: Ooooh. I think we've already begun.

BARNEY: I'll be down in a jiffy.

(BARNEY *disappears from the lighting booth. The actors begin speaking at once—ad libbing "He's crazy," "This is insane," etc.*)

PETER: When he opens the door, I want you to go. He could be dangerous. So, all of you—go. Get your things and go!

JOHN: Are you crazy? I wouldn't miss this for anything!

ACT TWO

PETER: John, go! All of you—the minute he opens the door, I want you to leave.

SALLY: *(As she and* MEG *cross)* He's deranged—that's what he is.

(There is the sound of a heavy chain being yanked on the other side of the door. The door immediately opens and BARNEY *is standing there, the chain hanging around his neck.)*

BARNEY: *(In a stage whisper)* I know who you are and I saw what you did!

MEG: Oh, please!

*(*BARNEY *suddenly pulls out a hammer from behind his back. The girls fall back, screaming.)*

BARNEY: FUCK OFF!!!!!

*(*JOHN *and* PETER *rush to the girls and pull them to one side.* MEG *breaks loose and runs straight towards* BARNEY.*)*

PETER: *(Catching her)* Meg!

*(*PETER *half carries her back to the others and amid much ad-libbing "Get us out of here," "He's got a hammer," etc.* PETER *manages to get them seated. Across the room,* BARNEY *is locking the door with the chain, fastening from the door handle to an adjoining pipe.)*

PETER: Relax. I know this game. I will win it in five minutes. Trust me. Can you trust me? All of you—I want you to trust me.

BARNEY: So we're playing this to the end, huh? 'Til one of us cries uncle?

PETER: Yes.

BARNEY: Who's going to keep time?

JOHN: I will.

PETER: We don't need a timekeeper. It won't take that long.

BARNEY: You're right. It won't. I can topple you in *five minutes!* Five minutes, John, five minutes!

(JOHN *nods and glances down at his watch.*)

PETER: Then I take it you're going to go first. And I trust you will try to be the master. *(Kneeling and throwing out his arms)* Lay on, MacDuff. I'm yours to command.

BARNEY: I know!

(*With the hammer brandished high,* BARNEY *strolls down the length of the room, eyeing* PETER *steadily. The others sit watching, riveted. Finally* BARNEY *pulls a chair over in front of* PETER *and places his foot on it.*)

BARNEY: Lick my boot. *(He grins at* ANNIE.*)*

(ANNIE *averts her eyes.* PETER *bends down and licks* BARNEY's *shoe. He licks one side and then the other. He licks over and over and over. Now he is holding on firmly to* BARNEY's *foot, caressing it, kissing it, causing* BARNEY *to tumble.* BARNEY *removes his foot from the chair but cannot dislodge* PETER. PETER, *still licking* BARNEY's *shoe, is dragged prostate across the room as* BARNEY *attempts to flee.*)

BARNEY: Let go of me!

PETER: I'm licking, master! I'm licking! Have you had enough?

BARNEY: Shut up, slave! Let go of me. Get over there.

(PETER *crawls back to his original position, pausing to smile at the three women, whispering.*)

PETER: Five minutes! Five minutes!

BARNEY: Shut up!

(BARNEY *spies the trash can by the door and drags it over to* PETER.*)*

BARNEY: Empty that!

ACT TWO 63

(PETER *empties the trash can. In the midst of assorted wads of paper, old coffee cups, etc., crusts of bread and several orange peels tumble out.*)

BARNEY: Aha! Someone's lunch. Why don't you have a little snack?

(BARNEY *touches a crust of bread with his shoe.*)

BARNEY: Eat that. Go on! Eat that! And that!

(PETER, *smiling, picks up the first crust of bread and takes a bite with relish. He finishes that crust and picks up an orange peel, holding it aloft before putting it in his mouth. He picks up another crust, another peel, growing more and more like an animal. He is wild. Still on his knees, he is advancing on* BARNEY, *still cramming handfuls of food into his mouth. He gets closer and closer to* BARNEY.)

BARNEY: Get back!

(*But* PETER *continues to advance until* BARNEY *is forced into a corner, against the far wall. Now* PETER *is chewing so fast the food flies out of his mouth and spews onto the floor.*)

PETER: *(With arms outstretched in victory)* I'm eating, Master! I'm eating! Just as you said!

(PETER *looks as if he will soon start biting* BARNEY. *He is unrestrained, over the top, crazed.*)

BARNEY: *KNEEL OVER THERE!!!!*

JOHN: *(Laughing)* Barney, I think you may have bitten off a little more than you can chew.

BARNEY: Oh, is that what you think?

(BARNEY *lunges at* JOHN *with the hammer, slamming it down on the table in front of* JOHN *with a vengeance. The girls cry out.* ANNIE *jumps from her chair and moves against the wall.*)

BARNEY: *(To* ANNIE*) Sit the fuck down!*

(ANNIE *slowly sits.* BARNEY *looks down at* JOHN *with the hammer poised above* JOHN's *head.)*

BARNEY: Slave! Why don't you tell John here why you enjoyed the kissing scene with him?

JOHN: What?

BARNEY: See, Johnny, he likes blondes just fine. But what he really likes is brunettes. Get it?

JOHN: No, I don't.

(BARNEY *brings the hammer down to* JOHN's *head, pushing it into his scalp until* JOHN's *head trembles.)*

BARNEY: He likes brunettes.

JOHN: What are you saying—that he's gay?

BARNEY: Nothing so mundane as that. He is everything to everybody, isn't he, Sally?

(BARNEY *has crossed behind the three women and he now bangs the back of* SALLY's *chair with the hammer. She jumps in terror.)*

SALLY: What do you mean?

BARNEY: You know what I mean.

SALLY: What?

(BARNEY *begins to comb the top of* SALLY's *head with the teeth of the hammer.)*

BARNEY: Like I said, he also likes blondes.

ANNIE: What is he talking about, Sally? Are you sleeping with Peter? Are you? *(To* PETER*)* Is she?

(PETER *continues to kneel across the room, watchful and silent.)*

SALLY: *(In tears)* Oh, yeah, sure. I'm sleeping with a man old enough to be my father!

BARNEY: *(Grinning at* PETER*)* Ouch! But wait, Sally, don't you have all those questions for Daddy?

ACT TWO 65

Sometimes rather late at night after everyone else is gone?

SALLY: Good God. So I asked some questions. He's the director, isn't he? This sucks!

(Behind BARNEY, JOHN *has slowly gotten to his feet, and is on his way towards* BARNEY. BARNEY *whirls quickly and steps behind* SALLY *with the hammer raised above her head.)*

BARNEY: *(Snarling)* Why don't you sit down.

PETER: *(Hissing)* John, sit. Sit!

*(*JOHN *sits.* SALLY *starts to weep uncontrollably.)*

BARNEY: Sally's sulking. Why don't you jolly her out of it, Meg? You really like Sally, don't you? Have you ever told Sally how much you *really* like her?

MEG: Sally, this guy is a creep. He's a sniveling, jackass, shithead, loser creep—

*(*MEG *rises out of her chair as if to attack* BARNEY. *He quickly moves in, swinging his hammer.* SALLY *and* ANNIE *grab her and force her back into her chair.* ANNIE, *still holding onto* MEG, *looks over at* PETER.*)*

ANNIE: Tell him to play the piano.

BARNEY: The piano?

ANNIE: Yes. Tell him to go over to the piano and sit down and play.

BARNEY: Go slave! Play for her now. *(He opens the piano bench and takes out the sheet music.)* Moonlight Sonata. *(Smiling at* ANNIE*)* I love that piece!

*(*BARNEY *places the sheet music on the music rack and then crosses to* PETER, *who is still kneeling, motionless.* BARNEY *yanks him by his hair and almost throws him onto the piano. There is a loud crash of keys.)*

PETER: Unfortunately, I don't play.

BARNEY: Aha!

PETER: *ON COMMAND! (Deadly)* Not for you. Not for anyone. I'm sorry that I have to disappoint you.

BARNEY: Play for her. If you don't, you lose.

PETER: But it's not your turn. What's the time, John?

BARNEY: It doesn't matter.

PETER: John, what's the time?

BARNEY: I gave you an order and you either wouldn't or couldn't play. So I won! Barney wins! *(Chanting loudly)* Barney beat Peter! Barney beat Peter! *(Laughing, to the others)* Can you say that? Can you say Barney beat Peter? Sally? Sally? Say "Barney beat Peter."

(BARNEY *moves over to* SALLY, *menacing her again with the hammer.* SALLY *is clearly traumatized.*)

SALLY: *(Sobbing)* Barney...beat...Peter...

BARNEY: Louder! I don't think he heard you. I said, louder! Say "Barney beat Peter!" I said—say...

(BARNEY *swings the hammer above her head.*)

SALLY: *(Almost screaming) Barney beat Peter!*

BARNEY: Thank you! That wasn't so hard! *(He crosses the room with great exuberance, kicking his foot in glee. Then, he quiets and kneels on the floor.)* I'm sorry. I'm not being a very good winner. Go ahead and take your turn.

PETER: Yes, my turn. Well, actually, I think this has gone far enough. I think we should stop.

BARNEY: That's what losers always say.

PETER: We've proven the point.

BARNEY: Now you're really grabbing at straws.

PETER: No, Barney, look at them. I think it's time you tell them who you are.

BARNEY: They know who I am.

ACT TWO

PETER: No, they don't.

BARNEY: Yes, they do.

PETER: Max, it's over.

(BARNEY *suddenly takes a breath and lowers his head.*)

JOHN: Oh, Christ.

PETER: That's right, John, this is Max.

(*The others watch in shock as* BARNEY *stands and moves to the back of the room and, during* PETER's *speech, he takes off first his jacket, then his cap, a fake moustache, his glasses, his cap, and finally his wig.* JOHN's *hair is close cropped and when he turns we see a man fifteen years older than* BARNEY, *one who is focused, intense, and quite handsome.*)

PETER: Max is the original member of this company. He followed me here from Australia and he's played a vital role. In the beginning he bound you all together out of sympathy for him. And now he's found your soft spots and torn you all asunder. He did it through his perception and his commitment and his gift. Of course, he's still a student. He still has much to learn—

MAX: (*With an Australian accent*) Oh, I don't know, I think I may have just graduated.

PETER: He's inclined to hit a little too heavy—

MAX: …summa cum laude…

PETER: There's a tendency to overdo—

MAX: Just don't forget, I won. (*Pause*) "Our fears in Banquo run deep…'tis much he dares…and under him my genius is rebuk'd; as, it is said, Mark Anthony's was by Caesar."

(MEG *is helping* SALLY *put her coat on.* JOHN *is gathering up her things.* PETER *senses this, turns, and begins to speak rapidly.*)

PETER: Of course you won, Max. Are you really that insecure? I hope not. I only stopped because the exercise was over, they witnessed the true intention. That was the purpose, remember? This was for their benefit, right, not yours? *(To the others)* Now, please, don't be intimidated by Max. Yes, he's formidable. But in the beginning he had his problems, too. For example, Max'd gone through life wondering if he was only accepted because of his money. I think to this day he still wonders about his real worth...after all, money buys a lot...

MAX: It bought you!

(PETER *springs forward, crosses the room to* JOHN, *and grabs him by the throat. They stand, eyes locked, frozen. The air is taut—the silence stretches. Then* PETER *suddenly embraces* JOHN *with great feeling.* JOHN *reciprocates. They begin to laugh.* PETER *is still laughing as he pulls away and spies the hammer.)*

PETER: Christ—a hammer? *(He picks up the hammer and exhibits it to the others.)* A hammer!

MAX: *(Still laughing)* Did you like that?

PETER: A little over the top, Banquo—

MAX: You think?

PETER: But good work. You were fierce. *(He turns to the others.)* Now, let's discuss—

(JOHN *has crossed to* PETER *and stands with his hand outstretched.)*

JOHN: Give me the key. Now.

PETER: The key! How apropos. Max, the key. Let him go.

(JOHN *goes to the door and unlocks the chain as* PETER *crosses to the girls.)*

PETER: But I want to talk to you, Sally and Meg—

ACT TWO

SALLY: You let him do this to me? Attack me? Humiliate me? He could have smashed my brains out! I'd like to smash your brains out! You are a monster! *(She suddenly grows calm.)* Get. Out. Of. My. Way. MOVE!!!!!!!!!!!!!!

(JOHN rips the chain from the door and throws it to the floor. MEG and SALLY cross towards him.)

PETER: Meg?

(MEG pauses at the door, distraught, in tears.)

PETER: MEG!!!!!!!!!!

(MEG cannot look at PETER. She glances around the room and sees ANNIE still sitting as if in a trance.)

MEG: Annie? Are you coming?

ANNIE: *(Almost mumbling)* I don't know what's going on.

(JOHN, MEG and SALLY glance at each other and exit. PETER follows them to the door and calls after them.)

PETER: It's a test. I'm testing you. I'm trying to find out if you can really do this work. I only ask of you what I demand of myself, but I ask for *all*!

ANNIE: There are voices screaming in my head. I must be crazy. And you call this a test.

PETER: It is. And so far the only one who's passed it is Max.

MAX: Now, don't go bragging.

ANNIE: It's cruel…twisted…

MAX: *(Gently)* Annie, there's a bigger picture. We give each other permission to go for the truth because we're here to create. Sally just lived one of the most important moments of your play. Isn't that why we're here, to make something live?

PETER: I told you all along it's about breaking boundaries.

MAX: I fancy a cup of coffee. Anybody else?

(ANNIE *glares at* MAX.)

MAX: Well, I'll be back in a bit.

(JOHN *exits.* ANNIE *stands and gathers her things.*)

ANNIE: I've got to get out of here. I think you're psychotic.

PETER: It's not for everyone.

ANNIE: It's not for anyone.

PETER: I'm trying to build a company. I have Max. Do I have you?

ANNIE: I'm getting out of here. I'm going to forget all about this.

PETER: But you won't forget, Annie. It will always tug at you. It will always whisper, "What if I'd stayed?" "What if I'd seen it through?" When some phony cast of actors is bullshitting their way through your play, you'll think of this. When you're sitting in the dark again, writing, and trying to say something that means something, you'll think of this. Any time you see pretense, any time you have anything at all to do with cowards who sidestep the truth, you will think of this and you will wish that you'd stayed. (*Pause*) But that, I guess, has always been the difference between you and me.

ANNIE: You are a monster. You are the devil incarnate.

PETER: We have a lot of work to do if egos aren't in the way.

ANNIE: Why don't you do this, Peter? Why don't you get on a plane and fly back to your ratty warehouse in Australia and get your ten people together and tell them. And don't forget Max! Make sure you take him!

ACT TWO

But just remember this. Everything you touch crumbles into dust...and will always crumble into dust. Not because you're so high and mighty artistic and so goddamned superior—no! It falls apart because there is something *deficient* in you. Something is wrong with you, Peter, and you hate that, don't you? And you don't know what it is, do you? Ooooh, did I strike a nerve, Mister DeMille? It bothers you, doesn't it? It just kills you.

PETER: That's good, Annie. You've struck a nerve, so keep going.

ANNIE: That's the way you work, isn't it? Find the wound and then pour on the gas. Well, that's the difference, Peter, between you and me. I refuse to do that. I won't. Not even to you.

PETER: You are so—fierce!! Don't go. I want you to stay.

ANNIE: No!

PETER: *(Stopping her)* Stay. Annie, with Max and you and me—we can finally begin. It can happen! We can create a real theater—the kind most people only dream about. And you can help temper me, soften me, make me more—

ANNIE: STOP!!!!

PETER: Because I care about you, Annie. You want the truth? Well, here's the truth. I care about you, Annie, and I don't want you to go.

ANNIE: Then play the piano for me. Play *Moonlight Sonata*. Play the third movement. I want to hear you play.

PETER: No. *(Pause)* I can't.

ANNIE: You can't or you won't?

PETER: I just...can't.

(ANNIE *turns and exits.* PETER *crosses the room and winds up sitting on the floor amid the rubber snakes and the remnants of food and trash. A moment later, outside the door, we hear footsteps.* PETER's *head snaps up. He waits for the door to open with a deep longing etched upon his face. He drops his head in disappointment as* JOHN *enters.* JOHN *is carrying a small bag from the deli. He opens the bag and takes out a package of crackers.*)

MAX: Petey want a cracker?

PETER: No, I want tea.

MAX: *(Taking out Styrofoam cups)* I brought you back a coffee.

PETER: I want tea.

MAX: *(Glancing at the littered room)* So much for that group. They're all gone.

PETER: Let's just wait and see. Let's just wait and see.

MAX: Whatever you say. *(Almost smirking)* You're the master.

(PETER *jumps up from the floor, grabs a nearby, chair and clangs it down with a fury. He slowly sits in the chair with the deliberation and arrogance of an emperor.*)

PETER: Get. Me. My. Tea.

(MAX *slowly backs out of the room, still smiling, and exits.* PETER *continues to sit in his chair, staring at the door, listening, waiting.*)

END OF PLAY

www.ingramcontent.com/pod-product-compliance
Lightning Source LLC
Chambersburg PA
CBHW071742040426
42446CB00012B/2439